DK Eye Wonder

Dinosaur

LONDON, NEW YORK, MUNICH,
MELBOURNE, and DELHI

Written and edited by Sarah Walker
and Samantha Gray
Designed by Janet Allis

Publishing manager Mary Ling
Managing art editor Rachael Foster
US editors Gary Werner and Magaret Parrish
Jacket design Chris Drew
Picture researcher Jo Haddon
Production Kate Oliver
DTP Designer Almudena Díaz
Consultant David Lambert

First American Edition, 2001

07 08 09 10 9

Published in the United States by
DK Publishing, Inc.
375 Hudson Street
New York, NY 10014

Copyright © 2001 Dorling Kindersley Limited

Library of Congress Cataloging-in-Publication Data

Gray, Samantha
Dinosaurs / by Samantha Gray and Sarah Walker -- 1st American ed.
p. cm -- (Eye wonder)
ISBN 978-0-7894-7851-1 -- ISBN 978-0-7894-8179-5
1. Dinosaurs--Juvenile literature. [1. Dinosaurs.] I. Walker, Sarah.
II. Title. III. Series
QE861.5 .G76 2001
567.9--dc21   2001017278

Color reproduction by Colourscan, Singapore
Printed and bound in Italy by L.E.G.O.

see our complete
catalog at
www.dk.com

Contents

4-5
What is a dinosaur?

6-7
Dinosaur times

8-9
Skeletons

10-11
Different dinosaurs

12-13
Dinosaur world

14-15
Little and large

16-17
On the move

18-19
Plant eaters

20-21
Hungry herds

22-23
Meat eaters

24-25
Pack hunters

26-27
Tough tactics

28-29
Camouflage

30-31
Courtship

32-33
Nests and nurseries

34-35
High flyers

36-37
Under the waves

38-39
Brain power

40-41
Death of the dinosaurs

42-43
Digging up dinosaurs

44-45
Building dinosaurs

46-47
Glossary and
Animal alphabet

48
Index and
acknowledgments

What is a dinosaur?

Dinosaurs roamed the Earth for over 150 million years, then mysteriously died out. These reptiles varied from fierce killers to gentle plant eaters. Lifelike models help us to imagine what they looked like.

Lizard legs

Like modern reptiles, most dinosaurs had scaly skin, a long tail, teeth, and claws. Today's reptiles have legs that splay sideways. Dinosaurs had straight legs directly below their bodies.

Sharp teeth lined the powerful jaws of many meat-eating dinosaurs.

Short arms were used for grasping prey.

Feathered friends

It is likely that not all dinosaurs died out 65 million years ago. Some small, feathered dinosaurs may have survived. Today's birds probably descend from them.

Birds have feet like those of many dinosaurs.

Motherly love

Clues to how dinosaurs behaved come from today's reptiles. Crocodiles are survivors from prehistoric times. They feed their babies and protect them. Some dinosaurs probably did this, too.

Creature features

Dinosaurs had different features to equip them for survival. Meat-eating dinosaurs had sharp teeth and claws for hunting. Some plant eaters grew to vast sizes. Others had natural weapons such as horns.

Some dinosaurs had a row of spines along their backs, from head to tail.

Large tail helped dinosaurs to balance as they leaned forward.

Most dinosaurs had bumpy, scaly skin.

Muscular hind legs allowed meat eaters to chase their prey.

Dinosaur facts

● Dinosaurs were the biggest land animals of all time, although some whales, such as the blue whale, are larger.

● Flying reptiles lived at the same time as the dinosaurs, but no dinosaur could fly.

● There were prehistoric swimming reptiles, but no dinosaurs swam in the sea.

Dinosaur times

The age of the dinosaurs is known as the Mesozoic era. This stretched from 248 to 65 million years ago. It divides into three separate time spans: the Triassic, the Jurassic, and the Cretaceous.

The Triassic period lasted from 248 to 206 million years ago.

Triassic world

At the start of the Mesozoic era, the continents were joined together into one supercontinent – Pangaea. This was surrounded by a massive ocean called Panthalassa.

Jurassic world

Over millions of years, Pangaea split into two continents, Gondwana and Laurasia. As these drifted apart, different groups of dinosaurs evolved on each continent.

Small beginnings

The Triassic world saw the first small dinosaurs. Like most early dinosaurs, meat-eating *Herrerasaurus* (he-rair-a-sore-us) walked on its hind legs.

The Jurassic period
lasted from 206 to
144 million years ago.

The Cretaceous period
lasted from 144 to
65 million years ago.

Cretaceous world

The continents continued to
drift apart and Earth began to
look like it does today. The vast
mountain ranges of the Andes
and the Rockies were formed.

Dinosaur heyday

The great variety of
Cretaceous dinosaurs
included horned plant
eaters like *Pentaceratops*
(pen-ta-serra-tops) and
huge meat eaters such
as *Tyrannosaurus Rex*
(tie-ran-o-sore-us recks).

Land of the giants

Late in the Jurassic period,
giant sauropods roamed in
huge conifer forests, while
Stegosaurus (steg-oh-sore-
us) ate low-growing plants.
Ichythyosaurs (ick-thee-oh-
sore-us) swam in the seas.

Skeletons

A skeleton tells a story. Teeth or bony beaks give information about what dinosaurs probably ate. Features such as horns show how they defended themselves. Small braincases tell us which dinosaurs had small brains!

Narrow jaw with sharp teeth

Small sprinter

A fossilized skeleton shows that *Coelophysis* (see-low-fye-sis) had long legs for its small size. Only 10ft (3m) long, it could run fast.

Spiky plant eater

A Late-Jurassic dinosaur, *Stegosaurus* (steg-oh-sore-us) was probably no more than 9ft (3m) high. It had bony plates along its back. Its spiky tail was flexible and most likely used for defense.

Bony plate

Small head

Long back legs

Short front legs

Tail spike

Tyrannosaurus rex could have swallowed a person whole.

Stiff, heavy tail helped balance

Large head with huge, hinged jaws

Powerful hind legs

Massive meat eater

Meat eaters like *Tyrannosaurus rex* (tie-ran-oh-sore-us recks) had massive jaws. They could open these extra wide to swallow large mouthfuls of flesh.

Long neck

Tail helped balance
while leaning
forward to sprint

Small head

Short arms

Birdlike dinosaur
A fossilized skeleton of *Struthiomimus*
(strooth-ee-oh-meem-us) shows that it
had features in common with today's
ostrich. These include a small head
with a narrow beak, a long neck, and
powerful hind limbs.

Long, strong
legs for running
at high speed

Jurassic giant
The longest of all the dinosaurs, sauropods like
Diplodocus (di-plod-o-kus) had small skulls containing
small brains! Despite its length, *Diplodocus* weighed
no more than two large elephants.

From head to tail, vast *Diplodocus* measured about 90ft (27.2m)

The sauropod's
skull is tiny
compared
to its body.

Long, stiff neck

Horned head
The Late Cretaceous *Triceratops* (try-serra-tops)
was hunted by *Tyrannosaurus rex*. It probably
used its horns to defend itself. A plant eater,
it had a tough, toothless beak.

Bony frill

Brow
horn

Nose horn

Wide rib cage
supported
bulky body

Short,
sturdy legs

Different dinosaurs

Dinosaurs are divided into two main groups, according to their hip bones. Some had hips arranged like a lizard's, and others had hips arranged like a bird's.

Lizardlike

This group includes two-legged meat eaters such as *Tyrannosaurus rex* (tie-ran-oh-sore-us recks) as well as plant-eating sauropods like *Diplodocus* (di-plod-o-kus).

Giant Saltasaurus (salt-tah-sore-us) lived in the Late Cretaceous period.

Bird bones

All bird-hipped dinosaurs were plant eaters. Some of the most familiar faces of the dinosaur world are found in this group!

Iguanodon (ig-wahn-oh-don) lived in the Cretaceous period. It grew to 30ft (9.3m) long.

10

- Strangely, experts think that today's birds evolved from lizard-hipped dinosaurs, not bird-hipped dinosaurs!

- To date, over 300 species of dinosaur have been found and named. Every few months more are discovered!

Tyrannosaurus rex *(tie-ran-oh-sore-us recks)* lived in the Late Cretaceous period. It stood over 20ft (6m) tall.

Gallimimus *(gally-meem-us)* lived in the Late Cretaceous period. It probably reached speeds of 43mph (70kph).

Triceratops *(try-serra-tops)* lived in the Cretaceous period. Its three sharp horns grew up to 3ft (90cm) long.

Stegosaurus *(steg-oh-sore-us)* lived in the Late Jurassic period. It had a toothless beak and a tiny brain!

Feeding on ferns

No grass grew in the prehistoric landscape. Instead, many types of ferns thrived on the forest floor. *Stegosaurus* (steg-oh-sore-us) munched on ferns and seed cones.

Dinosaur facts

● Duck-billed dinosaurs could chew through really tough plants because their jaws and teeth were so powerful.

● Flowering plants spread more quickly than other plants and soon became widespread throughout the world.

Dinosaur world

The dinosaurs' world was hot and sunny, like today's tropics. There were areas of desert, and forests of conifers and ferns. Later, the first flowering plants appeared.

Insect survivor
Some familiar insects fluttered in prehistoric skies. Modern dragonflies look very much like this fossilized dragonfly, which lived 140 million years ago.

Cycads
While dinosaurs ruled the world, palmlike plants called cycads were plentiful. They still grow in some parts of the world today, although they are rare.

Flower feast
Flowering plants, such as magnolias, first appeared in the Cretaceous period. They were probably eaten by plant-eating dinosaurs.

Prehistoric puzzle
Monkey puzzle trees thrived on Earth long before the dinosaurs. Today's monkey puzzles are related to these.

Mammal
One of the first small mammals, *Megazostrodon* (mega-zos-troh-don) lived alongside early dinosaurs. This furry model is based on a tiny skeleton.

Low life
Small meat eaters such as *Compsognathus* (komp-sog-nay-thus) hunted lizards and insects. They ran fast, chasing their prey through low-growing plants.

Mighty meat eater

Tyrannosaurus rex (tie-ran-oh-sore-us recks) was one of the largest meat-eating dinosaurs. It would have been tall enough to peer into an upstairs window.

Small but speedy

Compsognathus (komp-sog-nay-thus) was the size of a turkey. It may have been small, but its long legs meant it was built for speed. It could sprint fast after prey.

Little and large

Dinosaurs of many shapes and sizes roamed prehistoric Earth. They varied from small, birdlike dinosaurs to the most enormous creatures ever to live on land. Largest of all were the giant, long-necked sauropods.

Skyscraping sauropods
Huge sauropods such as *Barosaurus* (barrow-sore-us) could nibble leaves from treetops as tall as a five-story building. They were so massive that nothing dared to attack a healthy adult.

On the move

Dinosaurs are often thought of as lumbering creatures. Four-legged, heavy-footed types probably did move slowly, but there were also athletic dinosaurs. The fastest were probably the two-legged ornithomimids – the "ostrich mimics."

Plodding along

With their huge bodies and short legs, sauropods like *Saltasaurus* (sal-tah-sore-us) were among the slowest of the dinosaurs. They probably never moved any faster than people walk.

Gallimimus might have run at 43mph

Taking the fast track

Gallimimus, meaning "chicken mimic," may have been the speediest dinosaur. With its light body and long legs, it could sprint away from predators.

Fancy footwork

From footprints it is possible to see if a dinosaur was two-legged or four-legged. They also show whether a dinosaur was walking, trotting, or running.

Road runners

Like ostriches, *Gallimimus* (gally-meem-us) had powerful legs for striding out. Unlike ostriches they had long tails, which helped them to keep their balance.

(70kph), which is faster than a winning racehorse.

OOPS A DAISY!

It is not known if large, meat-eating dinosaurs could run fast. Their short arms could not break a fall if they lost their balance. An *Allosaurus* (allo-sore-us) found with 14 cracked ribs probably injured itself while running after prey.

Gentle giant

A huge sauropod, *Barosaurus* (barrow-sore-us) had a long, muscular neck for reaching food. It may have reared up on its thick hind legs to reach foliage high up in the treetops. A long tail helped it to keep its balance.

Plant eaters

Sauropods were the biggest plant eaters ever to walk the Earth. Most lived during the Jurassic period. Smaller plant-eating dinosaurs flourished before and after these giants existed.

Peglike teeth

Tearing teeth

For stripping leafy twigs, *Diplodocus* (di-plod-o-kus) had teeth right at the front of its jaws. Perhaps this sauropod ate conifers, cycads, ferns, and tree ferns.

Beak billed

Hadrosaurs (had-row-sores) had ducklike beaks for ripping up vegetation. They had more than 40 rows of teeth. They probably ate pine needles, seeds, twigs, and low leafy plants.

Strong teeth

Ducklike beak

Ground grazer

While sauropods munched treetop greenery, other dinosaurs tackled low-growing plants. *Edmontonia* (ed-mon-toe-nee-a) ate mainly ferns and mosses.

Dinosaur facts

- Herd dinosaurs probably had excellent eyesight, hearing, and sense of smell to detect danger.

- Hadrosaurs are also known as duck-billed dinosaurs.

- Herds may have been noisy. Calls to each other probably warned of nearby predators.

Forest friends

Giant herds of hadrosaurs, such as *Corythosaurus* (ko-rith-oh-sore-us), roamed through Cretaceous forests. They had hoofed fingertips for wading through swamps.

Duck-billed dinosaurs could store food in their cheeks, like hamsters.

Hungry herds

Some plant-eating dinosaurs formed herds. There was safety in numbers, and they could warn each other of predators. They may also have traveled together to find food.

Hiding in the crowd
Traveling as a herd makes it more difficult for predators to pick out just one animal. Today, as many as one million wildebeest herd together.

Some hadrosaurs had head crests in weird and wonderful shapes.

Warning call
The hadrosaur *Parasaurolophus* (pa-ra-sore-oh-loaf-us) had a long, hollow head crest. It probably blew through this to make honking noises. In this way it could warn the rest of the herd of any danger.

Horned defense
Herds could have used group defense tactics. *Triceratops* (try-serra-tops) may have formed a circle for protection, turning their horns outward to face an attacker.

Following the tail in front
Some herds of plant-eating dinosaurs may have trudged vast distances to find good grazing land. Herds of *Pachyrhinosaurus* (pack-ee-rye-no-sore-us) may have walked from Canada to northern Alaska each spring to feed on large-leaved plants.

Meat eaters

During the Cretaceous period, enormous, meat-eating dinosaurs ruled the land. Other creatures had to be on their guard against these ferocious hunters!

King of the reptiles

Tyrannosaurus rex (tie-ran-oh-sore-us recks) was one of the biggest meat eaters ever to live on Earth.

Dinosaur facts

● *Tyrannosaurus rex* had up to 60 teeth that were as long as knives, and just as sharp.

● The largest flesh-eating dinosaur was *Giganotosaurus* (jig-anno-toe-sore-us). This huge creature weighed an enormous eight tons!

Fearsome fish eater

Suchomimus (sue-koh-mime-us) was an enormous, fish-eating dinosaur with a head like a crocodile's! It probably waded out into rivers and lakes to catch fish with its jaws or clawed hands.

Long powerful jaws were lined with more than 100 razor-sharp teeth.

Crocodile smile

Like *Suchomimus*, *Baryonyx* (barry-on-icks), lived near water and ate fish. In addition to snappy jaws, *Baryonyx* had a large curved claw for spearing fish.

Scary skull

A relative of *Tyrannosaurus rex*, *Albertosaurus* (al-bur-toe-sore-us) was a frightening sight! It had enormous curved teeth and could move quickly after its prey.

HARD HEADED HUNTER!

Although *Tyrannosaurus rex* was a ferocious hunter, its huge size may have prevented it from running very fast. It is possible that *Tyrannosaurus rex* charged at and headbutted its prey to stun them. Then it probably used its short arms to grip its victims while it ate them!

Pack hunters

Some of the smaller, meat-eating dinosaurs snapped up prey such as lizards, small mammals, or eggs. Others probably ganged up in packs to overpower larger victims. Hunting in this way demanded teamwork and intelligence.

Sickle-shaped claw

Terrible talon

Velociraptor had a large, sharp claw on the second toe of each hind foot. Held off the ground for walking, the claw could sweep out like a switchblade knife to slash prey.

Pack attack!

Savage hunters, *Velociraptor* (vell-oss-ee-rap-tor) might have used group tactics to single out and attack victims. Raptors were well equipped to kill, with sharp claws, toothy jaws, and agile bodies. These intelligent dinosaurs may have circled and ambushed their prey as lions do.

Defend or die!

All was not over for *Protoceratops* (pro-toe-serra-tops). Its sharp beak was a useful weapon as it charged its enemy like a small rhinoceros.

Flexible neck for swooping down on prey.

Present-day packs

Today's pack animals perhaps hunt in the same way as *Velociraptor*. In a wolf pack, some members herd while others lie in wait to ambush prey.

Successful scavengers

Coelophysis (see-low-fye-siss) was a nimble, meat-eating dinosaur that lived and hunted in packs. They were not picky eaters and snapped up any creature they were able to swallow!

Dinosaur facts

- It is likely that *Velociraptor* used its muscular legs to stamp on small prey, like secretary birds do today.
- *Coelophysis* had hollow bones and was a light, agile, and speedy predator.
- *Velociraptor* and *Protoceratops* both lived during the Cretaceous era.

Tough tactics

Plant-eating dinosaurs were particularly at risk from predators. They needed protection from hungry meat eaters like this huge *Giganotosaurus* (jig-anno-toe-sore-us). Some had heavy coats of armor. Others made weapons of their claws, tails, or horns.

Dinosaur facts

● Lots of the smaller dinosaurs did not have methods of defense. If attacked, they would simply run away!

● *Ankylosaurus* (an-kye-low-saw-rus) was covered in armor plating. Even its eyelids were protected! Only its underbelly was free from protection.

Large, sharp teeth easily pierced the tough skin of victims.

Sharp thumb

Iguanodon
(ig-whan-oh-don)
was a peaceful plant
eater, but it
could use its
spiky thumb to
stab its enemy
if attacked.

Terrible tails

Euoplocephalus
(yoo-op-loh-sef-ah-lus)
probably swung its hefty
tail club from side to side.

*A Euoplocephales tail club
was a dangerous weapon!*

Whippy weapon

Barosaurus (bar-oh-sore-us)
may have used its long tail to
lash out at its enemies.

Barosaurus *could inflict a
stinging blow with its tail*

*Thin, bony plates
stuck up from
Stegosaurus's neck,
back, and tail.*

Plated protection

Stegosaurus
(steg-oh-sore-us) was
a huge dinosaur about
the length of a truck!
To put off predators,
it had very tough skin
and pointed, bony plates.

Markings break up an animal's outline so that they blend into the background.

Fading into forests

Large plant-eaters like *Iguanodon* (ig-whan-oh-don) probably had green scaly skin. Prowling predators would have found them hard to spot among the forest ferns!

Camouflage

The coloring of dinosaurs is unknown, but there are clues from today's animals. Dinosaurs were probably colored and patterned for camouflage in their habitat.

Did Velociraptor have green skin like iguanas?

... or pale skin with dark patches like leopards?

Lying in wait

Some meat-eating dinosaurs may also have had green or brown scaly skin. By blending into the background, they could sneak up on prey. See how this hunting crocodile looks like a log!

... or black stripes on reddish-yellow like tigers?

Predator in disguise

Velociraptor (vell-oss-ee-rap-tor) most likely had a leopardlike coloring. A light, sandy skin would match its desert habitat while spots broke up its outline.

Scaly story

Dinosaur scales did not overlap. They fitted together like floor tiles. Sometimes small scales surrounded larger ones.

Scales may have been different colors to form a pattern.

Beadlike scales vary in size and shape.

Looking leafy

Today's lizards also have scaly skins. Like *Iguanodon*, this iguana lives in leafy surroundings. Its emerald-green scales hide it from predators in its rain forest home.

Courtship

In the animal world, the strongest or most splendid-looking male has the best chance of attracting a female. Some dinosaurs may have challenged one another to trials of strength. Others showed off crests or frills.

Hard case

Pachycephalosaurus (pack-ee-seff-allo-sore-us), the "thick-headed lizard," had a dome of thick bone on top of its head. Maybe rival males head-butted or nodded to threaten each other.

A thick bony dome crowned the top of the head.

Rival males may have shoved each other to show off their strength.

Battle of the boneheads

In dinosaur herds, males faced a lot of competition to win a mate. The strongest males were most likely to be chosen to father young. *Pachycephalosaurus* males perhaps battled it out head to head.

Fantastic frills

Male *Pentaceratops* (pen-ta-serra-tops) had larger frills than the females. These were decorative, and males probably showed them off to attract a mate or to frighten rival males.

Spiky skull

The vast neck frill of the "spiked lizard" *Styracosaurus* (sty-rack-oh-sore-us) was fringed with six spikes. Males may have used these to impress females.

Nose horn may have been used for jousting with rival males.

Colorful crests

Corythosaurus (ko-rith-oh-sore-us) had tall head crests. These were hollow and helped produce trumpeting calls. Males' tall crests may also have scared off rival males and impressed the females.

Locking horns

Like some dinosaurs, some male mammals today seek to impress potential mates with displays of strength. Rams lock horns and try to push each other backward. The one losing ground finally slinks away from the winner.

Nests and nurseries

Like most reptiles, dinosaurs laid eggs.
Baby dinosaurs developed inside the
egg. Some dinosaurs were caring
parents. Others laid their eggs, then
left their babies to fend for themselves.

Eggs and nests

Lots of dinosaurs laid their eggs in nests. Some
nests were simple pits dug into the earth, while
others were built with mud. The egg shells were
brittle like those of birds' eggs, so that baby
dinosaurs could break through them to hatch.

Parental protection

This *Oviraptor* (oh-vee-rap-tor) died
wrapped around her nest. She may
have been trying to protect her brood.
It is likely that she was smothered by
wet sand. This probably happened
during a rainstorm more than
80 million years ago.

Young Leallynasaura
*may have squawked
to get their parents'
attention!*

Dinosaur facts

● *Maiasaura* (my-a-sore-a)
means "good mother lizard."
These gentle dinosaurs
carefully looked after their
babies when they were born.

● Some dinosaur eggs were
tiny, yet the babies often grew
into enormous creatures!

Happy families

Leaellynasaura (lee-el-in-a-sore-a) may have nested together in big groups like some seabirds do today. There is safety in numbers! After the eggs hatched the parents probably looked after their babies for several months. It is likely they kept them warm and protected them from predators.

Parents probably brought food for the baby dinosaurs

High flyers

While dinosaurs roamed the land, the skies were ruled by flying reptiles called pterosaurs. Large pterosaurs most likely flew over water, swooping down to catch fish. Smaller ones probably snapped up insects in the air.

Giant of the sky
The biggest flying animal that ever lived, *Quetzalcoatlus* (kwet-zal-koh-at-luss) may have weighed as much as a large human being. To support its weight, this Late-Cretaceous pterosaur had a wingspan like that of a light aircraft.

Soaring over the sea

Gliding over the Late-Cretaceous seas, *Pteranodon* (ter-an-oh-don) had no need to flap its wings once in flight. It had a long, bony head crest.

Bat wings

Like modern-day bats, pterosaurs had wings of leathery skin that stretched between their legs and finger bones. Their bodies may also have been furry.

Sky diving

A Jurassic pterosaur, *Dimorphodon* (die-morf-oh-don) flapped its wings to fly. It most likely skimmed the seas, maybe diving after fish like puffins do today.

Warm in all weather

To keep warm, the Late-Jurassic *Sordes* (sor-deez) seems to have had a thick, hairy coat. This is unusual for reptiles, which normally have scales, while mammals have hair.

Dinosaur facts

● The first-known bird was *Archaeopteryx* (ar-kee-op-terricks). It had feathers, wings, and a wishbone like a bird, but a reptile's teeth and bony tail.

● The modern-day hoatzin bird has claws on its wings. It uses these for climbing, like *Archaeopteryx* probably did.

● *Velociraptor* (vell-oss-ee-rap-tor) may have folded its arms sideways like wings. It may even have had feathers!

Under the waves

The world was much warmer when the dinosaurs lived, and there were no icebergs in the seas. No dinosaurs lived underwater, but prehistoric oceans brimmed with a variety of other weird and wonderful reptiles.

Speedy swimmer

Ichthyosaurus (ick-thee-oh- sore-us) means "fish lizard." These reptiles looked like dolphins but swam like sharks, flicking their strong tails from side to side. They gave birth to live young underwater.

Fearsome hunter

Liopleurodon (lie-oh-ploor-oh-don) had vast, powerful jaws that snapped shut on its unfortunate victims.

The enormous neck of *Elasmosaurus* grew up to 23ft (7m) long

Shark survivors

Sharks have existed for millions of years. They have swum in the world's oceans before, during, and after the time of the dinosaurs.

Giant sea serpent

Elasmosaurus (ee-laz-moe-sore-us) had two pairs of flippers. It flapped these like wings to glide through the water. Females probably came ashore to lay their eggs in the sand, risking dinosaur attacks.

"NESSIE," THE LOCH NESS MONSTER

People claim to have seen a sea serpent swimming in Loch Ness in Scotland. "Nessie" is described as looking like an *Elasmosaurus*. Whatever killed the dinosaurs killed *Elasmosaurus* too, but Loch Ness is very deep. Some people believe that Nessie hides in the depths.

Brain power

A simple way to measure intelligence is to compare the size of the brain to the size of the body. The brightest dinosaurs had bigger brains in relation to their body size than the less-intelligent dinosaurs.

Small head housed a small brain.

Modern mammals like the tiger are near the top of the class for animal intelligence.

Dinosaur dunce

Sauropods were among the least intelligent of the dinosaurs. They had vast bodies but tiny heads, with space for only a small brain!

Birds are next in intelligence to mammals.

Not so bright!

Dinosaurs most likely did not have the brain power of today's mammals and birds. Roaming Earth for millions of years, they still had enough brain power for successful survival.

Dinosaurs were less intelligent than today's birds.

Modern reptiles are less intelligent than some of the small hunting dinosaurs were.

The brightest of all

Compared to other dinosaurs, small hunters like *Troodon* (troh-o-don), had large brains in relation to their body size. *Troodon* probably used its intelligence to hunt in packs.

Dinosaur facts

● The size of a tall human being, *Troodon* had very large eyes. These helped it to hunt at dusk, and spot small prey.

● *Troodon* means "piercing tooth." It probably ate anything it could slash with its claws and tear apart with its teeth.

Death of the dinosaurs

Hundreds of different dinosaurs roamed the Earth 75 million years ago. Yet 10 million years later, all but their descendants the birds died out. What happened is still uncertain.

Huge hollow

An enormous crater hidden in the Gulf of Mexico was caused by a giant asteroid hitting Earth. The impact occured 65 million years ago, at the same time that the dinosaurs disappeared. It dramatically changed the Earth's atmosphere, and may well have led to the death of the dinosaurs.

The asteroid would have hit Earth at an incredible speed.

Deadly impact

The asteroid created a vast crater, similar to this one, when it hit Earth. Huge clouds of rock and dust blocked the Sun. These shielded out light and destroyed almost all plant life.

When this dinosaur died, it was quickly buried under layers of mud and river sludge.

Survival of the toughest

Some animals lived through the changes in the Earth's atmosphere. Scorpions, turtles, birds, and insects were just some of the ones strong enough to survive!

In time, the layers covering the dinosaur turn to rock. The bones become incredibly hard over millions of years.

The wind and rain wear away the rock. Scientists discover the dinosaur bones and begin removing them from their tomb.

Rare reward

Fossils are the remains of things that lived long ago. Dinosaur fossils are a rare find. They are usually found in rock layers that formed at the bottom of swamps, lakes, or rivers.

Over a long period of time, movements deep within the Earth force the skeleton toward the surface.

41

Buried bones

Removing dinosaur bones from a tomb of rock is a skilled job. Experts chip away carefully at the rock face to reveal bones that have not seen the light of day for millions of years.

Dinosaur facts

● The experts that dig up and rebuild dinosaur skeletons are called palaeontologists.

● Plant experts look for leaf remains in rock to learn about the prehistoric landscape.

● Fossilized droppings show what dinosaurs ate.

Digging up dinosaurs

Fossilized dinosaur bones can lie hidden in ancient rock. Dinosaur detectives, called palaeontologists, search for buried fossils. Sometimes they find fossilized bones, teeth, and footprints. The most exciting finds are whole dinosaur skeletons.

Plaster protection

Palaeontologists wrap bones in bandages and runny plaster. This sets hard, protecting the surface of the bone like plaster casts protect broken legs.

Careful cleaning

The bones are taken to a museum where the plaster is cut away. They may even arrive still inside the rock. Cleaning the bones is a skilled job.

Prehistoric puzzle

Rebuilding a prehistoric skeleton from a jumble of bones is a tricky task. It is like putting together a difficult jigsaw puzzle!

Palaeontologists piece together a Pliosaurus skeleton.

Building dinosaurs

Rebuilding a dinosaur is a lengthy process. Fossilized bones are removed from ancient rock. Experts then make a copy of these. Getting the replica bones ready for display is very complicated and can take a long time!

Making the mold
An expert begins by carefully painting each of the fossilized bones with liquid rubber. When the rubber dries, it makes a flexible mold.

Putting it all together
The molds are removed from the bones and coated in liquid plastic. This forms the outside of the replica skeleton.

Each limb bone is molded in two halves

Filling the bones!
Liquid plastic is poured inside the hollow molds. This sets into a stiff foam.

Finishing touches
The outer molds are removed to reveal the replica bones. They are pieced together and painted to look like real bones. The replica skeleton is then displayed for everyone to see!

Recreating the past

This lifesize copy of a *Barosaurus* (barrow-sore-us) skeleton is displayed in a New York museum. Metal rods are welded together to keep it in position. It is mounted on a supporting metal frame.

Guide ropes keep the replica steady as it is moved into position.

This replica is over 49ft (15m) high. It towers over visitors to the museum!

This Barosaurus is shown rearing up on its hind legs!

45

Glossary

asteroid A lump of rock that orbits the Sun.

camouflage Camouflage is usually skin coloring that makes animals look the same as their surroundings. This is to avoid being seen by predators.

carnivore An animal that eats the flesh of another animal.

conifer An evergreen tree that produces seeds in cones.

continent One of the Earth's great land masses.

crater A hollow in the ground, as caused by an explosion or an object from space hitting Earth.

Cretaceous The last period of the dinosaur age. It started about 140 million years ago and ended about 65 million years ago.

cycad A stumpy plant similar to a palm tree. Cycads and cycadlike cycadeoids were very common during the dinosaur age.

era A long stretch of prehistoric, or historic, time made up of periods.

evolve All living things change over long periods of time. These changes occur gradually over generations, allowing creatures to adapt to their surroundings.

extinction The death of a whole species.

fossil The preserved remains of a creature or plant that was once alive.

habitat The place where a creature or plant naturally lives or grows.

Jurassic The middle period of the dinosaur age. It began about 200 million years ago and ended about 140 million years ago.

mammal A warm-blooded animal with a hairy body and a backbone. Female mammals produce milk to feed their young.

migration The regular, seasonal journey of animals from one place to another to find food, warmer weather or to breed.

Mesozoic The age of the dinosaurs. This includes the Triassic, Jurassic and Cretaceous periods.

paleontologists Experts that dig up and rebuild dinosaur skeletons.

predator An animal that hunts another animal for food.

prehistoric Belonging to a time before history was recorded in written form.

prey Creatures that are hunted by other creatures for food.

reptile A cold-blooded, egg-laying animal that is covered in scales.

scale A small, thin plate that protects the skin of reptiles and fish.

scavenger An animal that eats the remains of a creature that another animal has killed.

species A group of animals or plants made up of related individuals who are able to produce young with one another.

Triassic The first part of the dinosaur age. It lasted from about 245 to 200 million years ago. Dinosaurs evolved toward the end of the Triassic period.

Animal alphabet

Every dinosaur and prehistoric creature featured in this book is listed here, along with its page number, its characteristics, and when it lived.

Albertosaurus 23
A two-legged meat eater.
(Cretaceous)

Allosaurus 17
A two-legged meat eater.
(Jurassic)

Ankylosaurus 26
A four-legged plant eater.
(Cretaceous)

Apatosaurus 19
A four-legged plant eater.
(Jurassic)

Barosaurus 15, 18, 27, 45
A four-legged plant eater.
(Jurassic)

Baryonyx 23
A two-legged fish eater.
(Cretaceous)

Coelophysis 8, 25
A two-legged meat eater.
(Triassic)

Compsognathus 13, 14
A two-legged meat eater.
(Jurassic)

Corythosaurus 20, 31
A two-legged plant eater.
(Cretaceous)

Diplodocus 9, 10, 19
A four-legged plant eater.
(Jurassic)

Edmontonia 19
A four-legged plant eater.
(Cretaceous)

Euoplocephalus 27
A four-legged plant eater.
(Cretaceous)

Gallimimus 11, 16-17
A two-legged meat eater.
(Cretaceous)

Giganotosaurus 22, 26
A two-legged meat eater.
(Cretaceous)

Hadrosaurs 19, 20-21
Plant eaters that could walk on two legs or four.
(Cretaceous)

Herrerasaurus 6
A two-legged meat eater.
(Triassic)

Iguanodon 10, 27-29
A two-legged plant eater.
It could run on two legs or walk on four.
(Cretaceous)

Leallynasaura 32-33
A two-legged plant eater.
(Cretaceous)

Maisaura 32
A two-legged plant eater.
(Cretaceous)

Oviraptor 32
A two-legged meat eater.
(Cretaceous)

Pachycephalosaurus 30
A two-legged plant eater.
(Cretaceous)

Pachyrhinosaurus 21
A four-legged plant eater.
(Cretaceous)

Parasaurolophus 21
A two-legged plant eater.
(Cretaceous)

Pentaceratops 7, 31
A four-legged plant eater.
(Cretaceous)

Protoceratops 24-25
A four-legged plant eater.
(Cretaceous)

Saltasaurus 10, 16
Four-legged plant eater.
(Cretaceous)

Sauropods 7, 9, 15, 16, 18-19, 38
Four-legged plant eaters.
(Jurassic, Cretaceous)

Stegosaurus 7, 8, 11, 12, 27
A four-legged plant eater.
(Jurassic)

Struthiomimus 9
A two-legged dinosaur.
It ate both plants and meat.
(Cretaceous)

Styracosaurus 31
A four-legged plant eater.
(Cretaceous)

Suchomimus 23
A two-legged fish eater.
(Cretaceous)

Triceratops 9, 11, 21
A four-legged plant eater.
(Cretaceous)

Troodon 39
A two-legged meat eater.
(Cretaceous)

Tyrannosaurus rex 7-11, 14, 22-23
A two-legged meat eater.
(Cretaceous)

Velociraptor 24-25, 29, 35
A two-legged meat eater.
(Cretaceous)

Other animals

Archaeopteryx 35
A prehistoric bird
(Jurassic)

Dimorphodon 35
A fish-eating flying reptile.
(Cretaceous)

Elasmosaurus 36-37
A fish-eating sea reptile.
(Jurassic)

Ichthyosaurus 7, 36
A meat-eating sea reptile.
(Jurassic)

Liopleurodon 36
A meat-eating sea reptile.
(Jurassic)

Megazostrodon 13
A tiny meat-eating mammal.
(Jurassic)

Pliosaurus 43
A fish-eating sea reptile.
(Jurassic)

Pteranodon 35
A fish-eating flying reptile.
(Cretaceous)

Pterosaurs 34-35
Flying reptiles that lived throughout the Mesozoic Era.

Quetzalcoatlus 34
A meat-eating flying reptile.
(Cretaceous)

Sordes 35
An insect-eating flying reptile.
(Jurassic)

Index

armor, 26-27
asteroids, 40-41

baby dinosaurs, 4, 32-33
bats, 35
beaks, 8-9, 19
bird-hipped dinosaurs, 10-11
birds, 4, 11, 33, 35, 38, 40-41
bones, 8-9, 41-45
brains, 8, 38-39

camouflage, 28-29
claws, 4-5, 24
colors, 28-29
continents, 6-7
courtships, 30-31
crests, 21, 30-31
Cretaceous period, 6-7
crocodiles, 4, 29, 36
cycads, 13

death of dinosaurs, 40-41
defenses, 21, 24, 26-27
dragonflies, 13
duck-billed dinosaurs, 12, 20

eggs, 24, 32-33
eyes, 20, 39

ferns, 12-13
flowering plants, 12-13
flying reptiles, 5, 34-35
footprints, 17
fossils, 41-45
frills, 30-31

Gondwana, 6

herds, 20-21, 30
hip bones, 10
horns, 5, 8, 21, 30

insects, 13, 41
intelligence, 38-39

jaws, 8, 12
Jurassic period, 6-7

Laurasia, 6
legs, 4
lizard-hipped

dinosaurs, 10-11
lizards, 4, 24, 29
Loch Ness monster, 37

mammals, 13, 24, 31, 38
meat-eating dinosaurs, 17, 22-25
    claws, 5, 23, 24
    colors, 29
    hunting, 13, 24-25
    teeth, 5, 23
Mesozoic, 6
monkey puzzle trees, 13
movement, 16-17

"Nessie", 37
nests, 32-33
noises, 20-21
oceans, 36-37

pack hunters, 24-25
palaeontologists, 42-43
Pangaea, 6
Panthalassa, 6
plant-eating dinosaurs, 13, 18-19
    colors, 29
    defenses, 26-27
    herds, 20-21
    size, 5
    teeth, 19
plants, 12-13, 19
predators, 21, 22, 27

reptiles, 4, 32, 34, 37

scales, 28-29
sea reptiles, 7, 36-37
sharks, 36
skeletons, 8-9, 41, 44-45
skin, 4, 27-29
stomachs, 19

tails, 4, 17, 27
teeth, 4-5, 8
Triassic period, 6

weapons, 26-27
whales, 5
wings, 34-35
wolves, 25

Useful websites

www.enchantedLearning.com/subjects/dinosaurs/
Everything you need to know. Lots of facts about all dinosaurs, plus quizzes, games, and printouts.
http://www.bbc.co.uk/dinosaurs/
Takes you on an interactive journey! Lots of fact files, games, and articles by experts.

Acknowledgments

Dorling Kindersley would like to thank:
Hilary Bird for preparing the index, Jon Hughes for digital illustrations, Andrew O'Brien for additional digital artwork p18, Clare Shedden and Mo Choy for design assistance, and Rachel Hilford for picture library services.

Picture credits

The publisher would like to thank the following for their kind permission to reproduce their photographs:
a=above; c=center; b=below; l=left; r=right; t=top;

American Museum Of Natural History: D Finnin 32tr; J Beckett 24tl. **Bruce Coleman Ltd:** Bruce Coleman Inc 16-17; Dr Hermann Brehm 10-11; Gerald S Cubitt 1tc; Gordon Langsbury 4tl, 5tl; Jeff Foott 31br; Jens Rydell 22; Jules Cowan 6tl; Pacific Stock 36bc; Tore Hagman 2tl, 3tr, 18. **getty images stone:** 14-15; Darryl Torckler 37. **Natural History Museum:** 17tl, 30tr, 31tr. **N.H.P.A.:** Daniel Heuclin 12, 24-25; John Shaw 28-29; Kevin Schafer 1c; Kevin Schafer 13br, 26; Martin Wendler 4bl, 5bl, 39. **Oxford Scientific Films:** 21tr; Daniel J Cox 25tr; Mark Deeble and Victoria Stone 4bl. **Planet Earth Pictures:** M & C Denis Huot 21cla. **Royal Tyrell Museum Canada:** 9tc, 9br, 10cb, 10c, 19br, 39crb. **Science Photo Library:** Francois Gohier 41tl; Jim Amos 42; Julian Baum 40tr; Peter Menzel 43c; Philippe Plailly 43tr, 43cla; Photo library International/ESA/SPL 40bl. **Senekenberg Nature Museum:** 8ca, 8c, 8-9cb. **State Museum of Nature** 8tr. **Woodfall Wild Images:** A Leemann 6bc; Alan Watson 20, 46tl, 47tr; Heinrich van den Berg 17tr; Ted Mead 29cla.

Jacket: **Bruce Coleman Ltd:** Bruce Coleman Inc front jacket/bc; Jules Cowan back cover. **Royal Tyrrell Museum Canada:** spine